Let's Read About Pets

Puppies

by JoAnn Early Macken

Reading consultant: Susan Nations, M.Ed., author/literacy coach/consultant

WEEKLY WR READER®
EARLY LEARNING LIBRARY

Please visit our web site at: **www.earlyliteracy.cc**
For a free color catalog describing Weekly Reader® Early Learning Library's
list of high-quality books, call 1-877-445-5824 (USA) or 1-800-387-3178 (Canada).
Weekly Reader® Early Learning Library's fax: (414) 336-0164.

Library of Congress Cataloging-in-Publication Data

Macken, JoAnn Early, 1953-
    Puppies / by JoAnn Early Macken.
      p. cm. — (Let's read about pets)
    Summary: Simple text and pictures briefly describe the physical characteristics
and behavior of puppies and how to care for them as pets.
    Includes bibliographical references and index.
    ISBN 0-8368-3801-7 (lib. bdg.)
    ISBN 0-8368-3848-3 (softcover)
    1. Puppies—Juvenile literature. [1. Dogs. 2. Animals—Infancy. 3. Pets.] I. Title.
SF426.5.M23   2003
636.7'07—dc21   2003045003

First published in 2004 by
Weekly Reader® Early Learning Library
330 West Olive Street, Suite 100
Milwaukee, WI 53212 USA

Copyright © 2004 by Weekly Reader® Early Learning Library

Editorial: JoAnn Early Macken
Art direction: Tammy Gruenewald
Page layout: Katherine A. Goedheer

Printed in the United States of America

1 2 3 4 5 6 7 8 9 07 06 05 04 03

Note to Educators and Parents

Reading is such an exciting adventure for young children! They are beginning to integrate their oral language skills with written language. To encourage children along the path to early literacy, books must be colorful, engaging, and interesting; they should invite the young reader to explore both the print and the pictures.

Let's Read About Pets is a new series designed to help children learn about the joys and responsibilities of keeping a pet. In each book, young readers will learn interesting facts about the featured animal and how to care for it.

Each book is specially designed to support the young reader in the reading process. The familiar topics are appealing to young children and invite them to read — and re-read — again and again. The full-color photographs and enhanced text further support the student during the reading process.

In addition to serving as wonderful picture books in schools, libraries, homes, and other places where children learn to love reading, these books are specifically intended to be read within an instructional guided reading group. This small group setting allows beginning readers to work with a fluent adult model as they make meaning from the text. After children develop fluency with the text and content, the book can be read independently. Children and adults alike will find these books supportive, engaging, and fun!

— Susan Nations, M.Ed., author, literacy coach, and consultant in literacy development

A newborn puppy cannot see. Puppies open their eyes when they are about ten days old.

A newborn puppy cannot hear. When they are older, puppies can hear much better than we can.

Puppies may have long hair or short hair. Puppies with long hair must be brushed more often. Some puppies must be clipped.

A playful puppy wags its tail. A puppy may whine if it is lonely or scared. It may bark as a greeting.

Puppies may growl as a warning. They may also growl when they play.

A puppy's baby teeth fall out, and adult teeth grow in. A puppy needs toys to chew on.

Be careful!
Puppies will eat
almost anything.
Give your puppy
fresh food and
water every day.

Pick a puppy that suits you. Some like to relax. Others like to run all day. Do you?

Glossary

clipped — cut off

growl — a deep sound made by an angry dog

sniff — to smell something

whine — a high crying sound

For More Information

Fiction Books

Schubert, Leda. *Winnie All Day Long*.
   Cambridge, Mass.: Candlewick Press, 2000.
Tuxworth, Nicola. *Puppies: A Very First Picture Book*.
   Milwaukee: Gareth Stevens, 1999.

Nonfiction Books

Driscoll, Laura. *All About Dogs and Puppies*.
   New York: Grosset & Dunlap, 1998.
Hodge, Judith. *Surprise Puppy!* New York:
   DK Publishing, 1998.

Web Sites
The 50 Most Popular Dogs in the US
www.enchantedlearning.com/subjects/mammals/dog/
popular.shtml
Printouts and brief descriptions of fifty popular dogs from
Enchanted Learning

Index

About the Author

JoAnn Early Macken is the author of two rhyming picture books, *Sing-Along Song* and *Cats on Judy*, and three other series of nonfiction books. She teaches children to write poetry, and her poems have appeared in several children's magazines. A graduate of the M.F.A. in Writing for Children and Young Adults program at Vermont College, she lives in Wisconsin with her husband and their two sons.